SMART CONTRACTS

THE ESSENTIAL QUICK & EASY BLUEPRINT TO UNDERSTAND SMART CONTRACTS AND BE AHEAD OF COMPETITION

GET YOUR SMART EDGE NOW!

VICTOR FINCH

AUVA PRESS

© Copyright 2017 Victor Finch - All rights reserved.

In no way is it legal to reproduce, duplicate, or transmit any part of this document in either electronic means or in printed format. Recording of this publication is strictly prohibited and any storage of this document is not allowed unless with written permission from the publisher. All rights reserved.

The information provided herein is stated to be truthful and consistent, in that any liability, in terms of inattention or otherwise, by any usage or abuse of any policies, processes, or directions contained within is the solitary and utter responsibility of the recipient reader. Under no circumstances will any legal responsibility or blame be held against the publisher for any reparation, damages, or monetary loss due to the information herein, either directly or indirectly.

Respective authors own all copyrights not held by the publisher.

Legal Notice:

This book is copyright protected. This is only for personal use. You cannot amend, distribute, sell, use, quote or paraphrase any part or the content within this book without the consent of the author or copyright owner. Legal action will be pursued if this is breached.

Disclaimer Notice:

Please note the information contained within this document is for educational and entertainment purposes only. Every attempt has been made to provide accurate, up to date and reliable complete information. No warranties of any kind are expressed or implied. Readers acknowledge that the author is not engaging in the rendering of legal, financial, medical or professional advice.

By reading this document, the reader agrees that under no circumstances are we responsible for any losses, direct or indirect, which are incurred as a result of the use of information contained within this document, including, but not limited to, —errors, omissions, or inaccuracies.

Trademarks:

Auva Press and the Auva Press logo are trademarks or registered trademarks and may not be used without written permission. All other trademarks are the property of their respective owners. Auva Press is not associated with any product or vendor mentioned in this book.

FIRST EDITION

ISBN-13: 978-1-5446-9150-3
ISBN-10: 1-5446-9150-5

Editor: Michelle Gabel
Cover Designer: Terrence Reese

To my loved ones and to friends,
who make my world more colorful

Abstract

The promise of smart contracts—enabled by the disruptive and revolutionary Blockchain technology—has been the subject of raging debate in a couple of industries. Experts believe that smart contracts hold the promise of curing problems associated with financial contracts, banking transactions, logistics, e-commerce, supply chain management and legal contracts.

It is a fact that reliance on traditional contracts—which uses physical documents—has led to delays in transactions, inefficiencies, and exposures to fraudulent activities. Employing smart contracts can help firms reduce risks, lower administration costs, and promote efficient business operations across multiple sectors of the economy.

The benefits of smart contracts will accrue from the revolutionary Blockchain technology, process reengineering, and changes in business models since t they allow transaction involving multiple parties. If you are a consumer, you are more likely to benefit from competitive services such as insurance policies and mortgage loans.

In addition, you'll be in a position to attain improved customer experience from deployment and adoption of smart contracts. However, to appreciate these benefits and develop better smart contract policies, both executives and customers have to answer the following key questions regarding smart contracts:

- What exactly are smart contracts?
- How smart contracts differ from traditional contracts?
- What are the major benefits of smart contracts in finance, legal, logistics, e-commerce, insurance and healthcare industries?
- How has the Blockchain technology facilitated the emergence of smart contracts?

- What are the main concepts of smart contracts programming?
- What is the future of smart contracts?

This book will focus on all aspects of smart contracts that you need to know to realize the true potentials of smart contracts and craft strategies. Welcome.

CONTENTS

Abstract **1**

Chapter 1 Introduction 3

Chapter 2 Innovative Disruption of Smart Contracts 13

Chapter 3 Resources for Smart Contracts 29

Chapter 4 Smart Contracts Programming Model 41

Chapter 5 Future of Smart Contracts 69

Chapter 6 Legal Perspectives of Smart Contracts ... 77

NOTES **82**

CONCLUSION **85**

ABOUT THE AUTHOR **87**

Chapter 1

Introduction

Welcome to the world of crypto-lawyers! This chapter explores all the basics of smart contracts. By the end of the chapter, you will be in a position to see the big picture of smart contracts. Let's get started.

What is a smart contract?

A smart contract can be seen as self-executing algorithmic code that's stored and replicated on a distributed ledger system—the Blockchain. The algorithm is executed by a network of nodes that run the Blockchain and can result in regular updates of the ledger.

In other words, a smart contract is a program that executes on the Blockchain when an action is triggered. For the program to run, many nodes need to verify it in the distributed network to ensure it is trustworthy. If you were wondering about the Blockchain technology and whether it is a trustworthy storage, you can be assured that smart contracts have the potential to provide trustworthy computations on the distributed storage.

As this might sound a bit confusing, let us clarify it. For instance, your bank behaves as smart contracts in some aspects. Let's assume that every month you have an automated payment, which deducts a regular amount of money and transfers it to your creditor. If the balance in your account is not sufficient to transfer the required amount to the creditor, the payment will fail.

In fact, you may get fined and another workflow will be triggered. These instructions are usually set by the bank. Your bank is the ultimate guardian of your bank account. The bank has complete control of your bank account details, and can arbitrarily alter the account balance. If this happens, you have to argue with them for the account balance to be reinstated.

What about smart contracts?

Smart contracts essentially can perform the verification of your bank account balance and transfer the money to your creditor.

With smart contracts, there is no need for a single source of control. Smart contracts use the Blockchain technology where several parties—autonomous computers—use a consensus mechanism to constantly check and re-verify any updates to the ledger. This promotes transparency.

Since all the nodes in the Blockchain network are running the same code, with each verifying the other, smart contracts will be visible to all. Any node can look into a smart contract and if it is satisfied with the logic, it can use it. On the other hand, if the node does not agree with the code, it does not run it. That is how transparency is promoted in smart contracts.

Traditional versus smart contracts

Traditional contracts are established through speeches, written words, and actions. These contracts form the key legal basis for private operators whenever they execute changes in their legal relations and try to prepare for future events. They also allow organized and collaborative actions that carry out economic activities.

Shared ledgers are useful when multiple parties in a transaction do not trust each other. For example, they are useful when two banks perform a complex derivative transaction with each other without the involvement of a third party such as a clearinghouse. In such a case, the transaction can only take place if the two banks trust that nothing that can forestall the transaction will happen.

However, this is not always the case. Parties may disagree on the outcome of the trade. What happens when parties do not agree on the outcome of the transaction?

Ideally, discrepancies can occur due to factors such as:

- Mutual misapprehension of initial trade requirements.
- Confusion arising from multiple copies of the original trade requirements when there are back and forth arguments with participating nodes protecting their interests.

- Disagreements regarding transactions that occurred in the external dependencies.

Smart contracts eliminate these challenges of traditional contracts. There is only one set of contractual terms that are written in a programming language. In the Blockchain, all the nodes agree with this code in advance. Such a contract can exist on the Blockchain and run whenever an event occurs. In this regard, smart contracts enforce the role of a trusted third party in contractual agreements.

In fact, smart contracts are not only about coding and automating of the contractual terms: they perform the role of a trusted third party by executing programmed tasks in the Blockchain ecosystem. The main objective of using Blockchain technology in smart contracts is to enforce "trust" through consensus and hashing algorithms.

The fact that all the nodes in the Blockchain technology can validate every row of smart contracts without needing a central validator makes them tamperproof from fraudulent activities and corruption. In this environment of "trust", smart contracts serve as a transparent means through which contractual terms can be enforced digitally.

By leveraging smart contracts, parties in a transaction will be in a position to promote transparency and flexibility with regard to contractual agreements. Nevertheless, one fact is certain: contracting in the Blockchain ecosystem is not only a matter of replacing conventional contracts with smart contracts. It certainly demands a combination of both traditional and smart contracts.

Such an approach should address the following issues:

- Practical challenges, technologies, risks, and operational processes of the Blockchain network.
- The importance of enabling ongoing changes and agility in a fast-paced and complex IT environment.
- The uncertainties and fears in the commercial world that include specific requirements for more complex commercial arrangements on the Blockchain platforms.

Table: Summaries of similarities and differences between traditional and smart contracts

The history behind smart contracts

In the year 1997, Nick Szabo, a computer scientist and cryptographer, coined the term "smart contracts" referring to a digitally signed and computable agreement between two or more parties. His research served as the basis for the current Blockchain-based smart contracts. Among many of Szabo's major contribution to smart contracts is the one that happened in 2002 when he created a language for contractual analysis.

This language established a bridge between legal terminologies and the procedural algorithms. By developing this language, Szabo was able to leverage the power of computation without leaving the nuances of legal technicalities. In October of 2008, a mysterious person by the name Satoshi Nakamoto published a paper titled: "*Bitcoin: A Peer-to-Peer Electronic Cash System.*" It is believed that an individual Satoshi Nakamoto does not exist, but that a group of scientists that discovered Bitcoin—the first cryptocurrency system —hides behind the name.

The discovery of Bitcoin has given birth to a variety of cryptocurrency systems such as Bitcoins, Litecoins, and altcoins. Nevertheless, it is not the Bitcoin cryptocurrency system that was revolutionary but the underlying technology—the Blockchain—that has facilitated the growth of new platforms such as real smart contracts. In the recent past, the majority of users outside of the technology field—such as players in the banking and finance sectors—have leveraged smart contracts in their business operations to increase efficiency and reduce costs.

Today, the scripting language used in smart contracts resembles Szabo's early programming efforts. However, the language has adopted a graphical approach with protocols such as Ethereum emerging as the best platform for the smart contracts development. The language of Ethereum protocol, the EtherScript, is graphical, modular and intuitive for the smart contracts development.

Thanks to Szabo and the Ethereum project, the smart contract technology has been availed. However, the technology itself does not create any obstacles. The true hindrances to the technology are the human-centered legal processes that are difficult to represent in smart contracts.

Chapter 2

Innovative Disruption of Smart Contracts

The possible uses of smart contracts extend far-off past the transfer of digital cash. Undeniably, smart contracts can be applied to business activities that involve purchases and exchanges of virtually any type of goods, services or rights, such as sales of commodities, personal properties, and digital rights. Gaze into the future, and you can see the innovations of smart contracts.

However, before we begin to explore the uses of smart contracts, let us first discuss advantages and disadvantages of smart contracts.

Merits and Demerits of smart contracts

Just like any technology, smart contracts have their own advantages and disadvantages. Let's get started and learn about the merits and demerits of smart contracts.

Merits of smart contracts

Smart contracts have the following benefits:

#1: Minimized risks

The distributed process of running transactions eliminates the risk of manipulation since the whole Blockchain network, rather than an individual node, manages every execution automatically.

#2: They provide real-time and accurate record of trade

Smart contracts use algorithms that automate tasks that would otherwise be performed manually. Thus, they increase the speed of business operations and are less susceptible to manual errors.

#3: They have fewer intermediaries

They reduce intermediaries. In some instances, they can eliminate reliance on third-party companies that provide 'trust' services such as the Escrow between trading parties.

#4: They have lower costs

Because of no human intervention, smart contracts have reduced costs.

#5: New business models

Smart contracts facilitate new kinds of business models such as automated access to vehicles and storage units.

Demerits of smart contracts

Below are some of the disadvantages of smart contracts:

#1: Still not accepted by majority of people

Despite the benefits, smart contracts are still not widely accepted by the majority of people. Only a small group of users has accepted smart contracts as a digital platform for enforcing contractual terms and agreements. This makes it difficult to depend on them completely as contractual terms enforcements.

#2: The credentials of users can be lost

What happens if the hard disk that stores the smart contract code becomes corrupted or crashes? In that case, all the details of the smart contract are completely lost. In such a scenario, you cannot do anything to recover it.

#3: Inherent risks in the technology

There are still inherent risks of unknown technical flaws in smart contracts. In addition, there are certain legal challenges that are associated with the implementation of smart contracts in highly regulated industries such as financial services industry, which may hinder its adoption.

#4: There is no physical form

Let's face it—we are used to traditional contracts that we can see. This is not something that characterizes smart contracts. Still, a number of challenges are associated with execution of smart contracts in the public sphere. For instance, transferring access to physical products using smart contracts may demand a digital chip, which now still does not exist.

#5: Difficult to enforce in a court of law

Because computer algorithms are responsible for the contract, it is difficult to prove its validity and accountability in any court of law.

Smart contracts' Use Cases in Industries

Smart contracts are still at their infancy stage. Therefore, business and technology enthusiasts who are interested in staying current on the implications of the technology should track both technology and its uses in industries. Below you can find several smart contracts uses in various industries.

Banking

The Blockchain used in smart contracts provides a single immutable ledger as the source of data. Smart contracts can provide firms with capabilities of automated workflow approval and clearing calculations. This can potentially eliminate all errors, lessen the costs and reduce the time of payment settlement. It is a fact that the process of bank clearance and settlement entails labor-intensive activities such as approvals and complex reconciliations. Smart contracts can eliminate these challenges.

By converging other revolutionary technological approaches (big data, robotics, and cloud infrastructure) with smart contracts, the benefits can be substantial.

One potential bank that could stands to benefit is JPMorgan Chase & Co. With their new learning machine, called COIN (Contract Intelligence – launched in June 2016) does the mundane, yet important and time-consuming job of interpreting commercial-loan agreements. This mean beast consumes 360,000 hours of work each year by loan officers and lawyers in seconds with lesser errors and work 365 days without break.

Could you imagine how disruptive it could be if this mean machine is enhanced with Smart Contracts?

This is just the beginning...

Finance

Banking institutions can leverage smart contracts to provide an accurate and transparent recording of their financial data. The fact that smart contracts allow data to be appended to the block in a transparent manner makes them perfect for uniform storage of financial data across multiple banks at reduced costs. Among the benefits that are likely to accrue from banks using smart contracts are:

- Increased transactional data transparency and integrity, which is necessary for financial market stability.
- Reduced expenditure of accounting information system storage through cost sharing across multiple banking institutions.
- Improved and better insights into client's capital because of increased financial accessibility.

Stock, Commodities, Option Trading

Smart contracts can facilitate simplified and efficient international transfers of goods and services through a faster letter of credit, which can be programmed as a smart contract, and trade payment initiation while providing higher liquidity of the financial assets. Smart contracts enabled payment approaches and automated processes that improve the process of financing.

The benefits that accrue from using smart contracts in the banking are multifold. One, there is enhanced approval and payment initiation which is enabled through the automated compliance and monitoring of letter of credit contractual terms. Two, there will be enhanced efficiency in the process of creation, modification, and validation of the trade. And, finally, there is improved liquidity of financial assets, which is created through the ease of transfer and fraud cutbacks.

Supply chain management

Smart contracts can provide the necessary visibility that is required at every step of a supply chain. IoT devices can append their agreements to a smart contract as the product is shifted from the factory floor to the shelves in real-time. This enhances the transparency of products movements. Among the benefits of using smart contracts in supply chain management are:

- The delivery of complex multi-party systems is simplified.
- Granular-level inventory tracking and delivery assurance are achieved, therefore improving the supply chain financing and risk management.
- Tracking and verification of products are improved to reduce risks and fraud.

Healthcare

Clinical trials can benefit from the smart contracts through improved cross-institutional research and visibility. The fact that these contracts can provide a privacy preserving computation means that sharing and tracking of patient data between healthcare institutions during clinical trials will be possible.

Because of improved sharing of patient data, smart contracts may provide the following benefits:

- Improved visibility and reduced costs through streamlining of the setup processes for clinical trials.
- Increased access to cross-institution patient data in case of an outbreak of epidemics where data is protected by the privacy-preserving computational algorithms in the Blockchain.
- Improved automation in the processes of obtaining and tracking consent for shared access to patient data.
- Increased confidence in the patient privacy with regard to data sharing.

Insurance

Smart contracts can be used in the auto insurance industry. Currently, the process of claiming from insurance companies in the case of car accidents is disjointed. The process can be improved significantly through smart contracts. Smart contracts can be used to record the policy, driving records, and drivers' reports. With recorded data, IoT equipped vehicles can execute initial claims in case there is an accident.

Such a system can have several advantages that include:

- A Central repository of data for each policyholder. Such data may include the global driving record, the policy, the type of vehicle, and the accident report history.
- Damage assessment report for each vehicle using sensors that can execute initial insurance claims and police reports

- Improved savings through reductions in duplicated work of verifying reports and policies.

E-commerce

Smart contracts can alter all the processes involved in online shopping. In the current scenario, a user has ordered for goods and paid upfront for the delivery of goods. Of course, payment is done using the conventional payment gateway systems such as PayPal, Skrill, and EFTs. But we all know the pitfalls of these systems.

Besides the high transactional costs in the form of merchant—third party systems—and lengthy times for goods or services to be delivered, a system that ensures goods to be delivered to the buyer is not in place. What happens if you pay for goods and services, and the seller does not ship them?

The majority of buyers have been using escrow services to eliminate these challenges. However, these services add extra costs to transactions.

Smart contracts can be used to serve as escrow services in e-commerce. Under the smart contract approach, payment of goods and services is withheld until the goods are actually delivered. The contract can only be fulfilled when payment has been released to the sender.

An example of an application that uses smart contracts is the Uber. The Uber transport system is run through a smart contract where the contract starts when you agree to be picked up from your current location and be driven to another. When all the requirements of the Uber driver have been met and you have been dropped at your destination, the contract is automatically triggered and payment is made.

IoT

As Blockchains and cryptocurrency systems proliferate, there are several crucial implications for IoT and the creation of smart systems. For one, the Blockchain technology could provide a mechanism for tracking unique history of the IoT individual devices recording them on the Blockchain and monitoring the exchanges between them and other devices, internet services, and other human users.

Smart contracts could also allow smart devices to become self-governing agents. Such agents could autonomously conduct a variety of transactions in the smart contract ecosystem. Just imagine a vending machine that can monitor and report its own levels of stock and also solicit bids from the distributors and automatically pay for them when delivered.

Alternatively, envisage a suite of smart devices such as home appliances that can bid with each other for priority so that the dishwasher, the laundry machine, and the robo-vacuum all run at an applicable time while minimizing the cost of electricity.

Ideally, smart contracts have the potential to allow smart devices become independent agents—DACs

(Distributed Autonomous Corporations), as referred to by some experts. Such agents will find their applications in wide a variety of industries ranging from electronic couriers to escrow services and auto-installation services.

Chapter 3

Resources for Smart Contracts

After understanding the basics of smart contracts, it's now time to explore the technology that is fueling smart contracts. By the end of the chapter, you will be in a position to explain how smart contracts work. Let's get started.

Blockchain technology

The Blockchain—the underlying technology behind the Bitcoins— is a decentralized ledger of records. The initial objective of Blockchain technology—which is now called Blockchain 1.0— as envisioned by Satoshi Nakamoto, was to allow trusted financial transactions between any two or more parties without the need for a trusted third party.

In fact, when Satoshi Nakamoto conceived Bitcoin in 2008, he did not use the word Blockchain but he laid its foundation by striving to prevent the "double spend" problem. The "double spend" problem is a problem that arises when two or more parties spend the same amount of currency without the need for a trusted third party.

To solve the "double spend" problem, he proposed the following requirements which laid the foundation for Blockchain 1.0:

- To all the participants in the Blockchain, nodes are required publicly to "announce" all their financial transactions or changes they make to their documents.
- Developing a system that allows all the nodes to "agree" on the transactions that are appended to the Blockchain.

It is the second requirement that gave rise to Blockchain 2.0 that is disrupting the normal world order. In the past seven years, Blockchain 2.0 has been extended from cryptocurrency systems to other types of records such as Ethereum and smart contracts, which create a cross-industry open standard platform for distributed ledgers.

At some point, we have all used ledger books. One such common feature of a manual ledger book is the ability to facilitate the transfer of chronologically stored journal entries of a particular type. For instance, your ledger can be made to store information about assets of your organization. These may include cash, inventories, investments, receivable accounts and equipment.

Data is appended on the Blockchain-based on cryptographic protocols. You can think of cryptographic protocols as some form of data abstraction from malicious users in the Blockchain ecosystem. In particular, the cryptographic protocols scramble or encrypt the data that is exchanged in the Blockchain network to ensure that party tampers with the Bitcoin transactions.

Net benefits of using these protocols are to ensure that old records are maintained and stored forever while new ones are appended to the Blockchain irreversibly. To promote transparency of transactions storage, all the Blockchain parties in the Blockchain network can view the same transaction history. Since Blockchain is distributed, every user in the network will have a stored copy of all the transactions on his/her hard disk.

Briefly, the Blockchain can be conceived as an independent, immutable, and permanent distributed database that coexists on multiple servers that are shared by the Blockchain community.

For more information on the Blockchain technology you can read my latest book: "Blockchain Technology: The Essential Quick & Easy Blueprint To Understand Blockchain Technology and Conquer The Next Thriving Economy! Get Your First Mover Advantage Now!" available in Amazon.

Digital Platform and Boundary Resources

Digital platforms have shifted the boundaries for the majority of industry ecosystems, changing how value is captured and creates, in addition to changing job descriptions and trust relationships between different entities in the economy. Making predetermined boundary resources available to any person who wishes to participate is a noble strategy in platform innovation management.

What exactly are digital platforms?

The term "digital platforms" refers to IT systems through which different parties can conduct business, which adds value to the whole Blockchain network. Parties can be users or suppliers of the IT platform or any inter-organizational interest groups that include application developers or advertisers.

In the context of smart contracts, different parties can create, provide, and maintain complementary services through various distribution channels and markets, while sticking to the agreed algorithmic rules and user experiences. In particular, platforms must commit and attract different parties with financial incentives generated by the smart contracts network.

The net effect of digital platforms on smart contracts and technological compatibilities is best demonstrated by the boundary resources. Boundary resources are simply contractual rules coupled with tools and boundaries that provide an interface between the digital platform company and third parties.

It is typical for digital boundary resources to be openly available and free—open source—for any third party that is on the web. Such arrangements provide a heterogeneous population of users that participate in the development and maintenance of various digital platform services and their system architectures.

Boundary resources can be best understood as the opposite of barriers to entry of other applications. They lower the often-large development and commercialization costs that are related to innovations. As a result, they help in creation of wider networks in the Blockchain ecosystem. One way to view the Blockchain technology is as something a technology that enables the development of next generation of digital platforms and their corresponding boundary resources. Characteristically, digital platforms have always been viewed as vendor-specific platforms or platforms that are controlled by a certain central operator. That is not the case with the Blockchain technology. Being a distributed system, Blockchain is maintained by a multitude of autonomous parties.

Smart Contracts explained

While the Blockchain technology was conceived in 2008 as the underlying technology of Bitcoin, it is only Ethereum that has popularized the concept of smart contracts. Ethereum is a public, open-source, Blockchain-based decentralized computing platform that features smart contracts' scripting functionality. It remains a puzzle why Bitcoin cannot provide the same range of functionalities as Ethereum.

However, despite the fact that Ethereum currently provides more flexibility with regard to programming languages used in smart contracts

(Ethereum was created with developers in mind), the two Blockchain-based platforms can provide the same smart contract development functionality.

The source code for Bitcoin was implemented in C++. Therefore, coding for Bitcoin applications often happens at a more granular layer. The net effect of granular programming is that it makes the platform less desirable for development of many new-age web-based systems. However, the high-level languages that are readily available within Ethereum ecosystem make smart contracts accessible to most developers.

For instance, Geth—which is implemented in Go—is available to Ethereum developers and can be used to encode complex smart contracts in a simplified manner.

How do smart contracts work?

Ethereum developers can load smart contracts into their Blockchain system through a transaction to the Blockchain network which has a payload. The payload contains the main logic of the contract. During the transmission of a transaction, it is not sent to a specific address. Instead, the autonomous nodes in the Blockchain network automatically recognize any smart contract payload (remember the payload has the smart contract logic) and generate a smart contact address.

Now, once uploaded to the Blockchain network, with the preconditions that are necessary to trigger it, the payload is activated by sending it to its specified address. When the smart contract is triggered, it can lead to sending other transactions that, again, trigger other contracts. Theoretically, the process can continue indefinitely.

What about Bitcoin's smart contracts?

Each transaction exists on the Blockchain as a data structure with inputs and outputs. For the Bitcoin to be sent, smart contract users must provide certain input requirements that can be proved and are predetermined. Smart contract users can also develop their contract code transactions with a complex set of inputs that trigger the Bitcoin on the Blockchain.

For instance, the multi-signature transaction can be viewed as a complex input that requires multiple parties to sign the data for the transaction to be triggered. Such an arrangement is similar to an escrow service where two or more persons are required to trigger a transaction.

One of the most abstract implementations of smart contracts in Ethereum is the DAO (Decentralized Autonomous Organization), which in the interconnected web of smart contracts has multiple payloads and embedded rules. In May 2016, the DAO raised a whopping $160 million, which is one of the world's largest crowdfunding until now. This roughly demonstrates the power of smart contracts.

The next chapter explores steps required for you to begin implementing a smart contract.

Chapter 4

Smart Contracts Programming Model

The main objective of this chapter is to teach you everything you need to know about smart contracts programming with Ethereum. By the end of the chapter, you will be in a position to develop your own smart contract and any decentralized app. However, before we get started, why should you select Ethereum and not Bitcoin as your digital platform?

That is a good question.

Both are based on the Blockchain technology. However, Ethereum is more than just a cryptocurrency. It is a decentralized cryptocurrency system that uses its inbuilt currency—the Ether—as a fuel for powering the programmable smart contracts that are executed on the Blockchain.

The source code for Bitcoin was implemented in C++. Therefore, coding for Bitcoin apps often happens at a more granular layer. The net effect of granular programming is that it makes the platform less desirable for development of many new-age web-based systems. However, the high-level languages that are readily available within Ethereum ecosystem make smart contracts accessible to most developers.

For instance, Geth—which is implemented in Go—is available to Ethereum developers and can be used to encode complex smart contracts in a simplified manner. In other words, Ethereum is a more expanded form of Bitcoin but built with smart contracts in mind and not just as a cryptocurrency system.

That is why any developer interested in the development of smart contracts should consider Ethereum.

Ethereum Virtual Machine

Ethereum is a programmable Blockchain system. It provides a set of pre-defined operations—similar to those in bitcoin transactions—and allows you to develop your own operations of any magnitude and complexity. Ideally, Ethereum serves as a digital platform for the development of decentralized applications, including cryptocurrency systems as well as others.

In particular, Ethereum was invented with smart contracts in mind. At the heart of Ethereum is the Ethereum Virtual Machine, which is simply abbreviated as EVM. EVM can execute any smart contract code of any arbitrary algorithmic length and complexity. In technical terms, EVM can be perceived as a complete "Turing machine".

The Turing machine can be perceived as the "world computer", where a developer can create applications and run them on EVM using friendly programming. For instance, you can create smart contracts and execute them on EVM using programming languages such as Python, Go and JavaScript. Sounds interesting, doesn't it?

Additionally, just like any Blockchain-based system, Ethereum also uses a peer-to-peer network protocol, where the Blockchain database is supported and updated by multiple autonomous nodes that are connected to the Blockchain network. Each and every node of the Blockchain

SMART CONTRACTS

network must run the EVM and execute the same smart contract instructions.

Now, to begin developing your smart contracts, you will need a client which is connected to the Ethereum network. The client will serve as a window to the distributed Blockchain network and provide a view of the Blockchain—where the EVM has been installed.

You can use either Pyethereum or Dapps a platform for executing your smart contracts. Let's dive in and explore these libraries.

Pyethereum

Pyethereum is the Python-based core library for implementation of Ethereum smart contracts. It provides the basic classes and necessary routines for interacting with Ethereum smart contracts. We have made a virtual machine that contains all the necessary software. In particular, Pyethereum allows you to interact with the Blockchain, test, and run your smart contracts.

Pyethereum is a Python-based ethereum client system. But it is not the only one available. Today, there are Ethereum implementations in C++ (CPP-ethereum) as well as Go (go-ethereum or simply Geth). At the most basic level, all you need to begin using Pyethereum is the latest OS (whether Windows, Linux or Macintosh), Pyethereum, and the latest version of Serpent.

I know, now you are wondering what is Serpent.

Serpent is a high-level programming language that can write Ethereum smart contracts. As the name suggests, it has been designed around Python programming syntax. However, Serpent is meant to be optimally clean and simple. It combines the benefits of efficiency advantages that result from low-level features and ease-of-use.

It allows you to compile your serpent code into the stack-based form and execute it on the Blockchain. In addition, while providing efficiency during programming, when compared to Python, Serpent has the following key distinctions:

- While Python integers have an unlimited size, the Serpent integers go up to 2256.
- While Python program allows decimals, Serpent does not support decimals.
- Python compiler supports lists, dictionaries, and other advanced data structures while Serpent has no such lists.
- Python compiler supports first-class functions while Serpent does not.

Dapps

A Dapp is a service that allows direct digital interaction between the end users and the providers. For instance, a Dapp can digitally link buyers and sellers in a marketplace. Ethereum Dapp's user interface is implemented in HTML using the JavaScript API framework to communicate with the Blockchain.

These frameworks provide the basis upon which Dapps append transactions on the Blockchain. Characteristically, Dapps have their own suite of associated smart contracts on the Blockchain that encode the business logic and provide tenacious storage of their consensus-critical state. The decentralized services that Dapps provide include financial and insurance services, social networks, prediction markets, gambling services, marketplace, IoT, governance, and games.

Ethereum facilitates the development of decentralized web that is commonly referred to as "web 3.0."Web 3.0 applications are different from web 2.0 applications with which you are familiar. What makes these applications different from the conventional web 2.0 is that they do not require any web servers as they rely on the Blockchain technology for execution.

Essentially, a Dapp has two main parts: the front-end that is written in HTML and the backend that forms the database. The good news is that if you know bootstrap or how to develop a web application in any framework, you will continue to use them as your front end. In fact, the process of creating a front-end for Dapp is the same as website development.

Moreover, you will get any reactive programming included in Dapp development by simply using the callback function, so there is no need to learn a new development framework. However, these applications will be executing differently from the conventional web 2.0 ones. Ethereum system depends on cryptographic algorithms to function. Therefore, every Dapp must know the identities of the others in order to communicate.

This means that you will not be creating accounts for users to log in and access Dapps. You can think of this phenomenon as "Open ID by default." The only issues regarding these systems are with the dishonest users who can exploit them for the development of gambling sites by falsifying cryptographic details to make a quick buck.

Dapp development requires a solid understanding of the following developer tools:

- ***Web3 JavaScript API***. It is the main JavaScript SDK that provides an interaction with all the Ethereum nodes in the Blockchain.
- ***JSON RPC API***. It is a low-level JSON RPC 2.0 interface to interface with Ethereum node on the Blockchain. It is used by the Web3 JavaScript API.
- ***Solidity Docs***. It is the programming language which has been developed for Ethereum smart contracts. It helps to compile Ethereum smart contracts to EVM opcodes.
- ***Solium***. It is a linter for the Solidity language that adheres to rules prescribed by the official Solidity programming style guide.
- ***Test Networks***. The test networks help smart contract developers to create and test their codes and network interactions

without spending their ether on the main Blockchain network.

Dapps can also be implemented in IDE frameworks. Below are developer frameworks and IDEs that you can use for writing your Ethereum smart contracts:

#1: Truffle

Truffle is an IDE that provides the testing framework and the asset pipeline for Ethereum smart contracts.

#2: Dapple

A dapple is a tool for the Solidity programmers that help to build and manage very complex smart contract systems on the Ethereum Blockchains.

#3: Populus

Populus is a smart contract development framework that is implemented in Python.

#4: Eris-Package Manager

The Eris Package Manager helps to deploy and test smart contract codes on private and public Blockchains.

#5: Embark

Embark is a Dapp development framework that has been implemented in JavaScript.

Setting up Pyethereum

To begin using Pyethereum, you should ensure it is installed along with the Serpent. But before you install these applications, git has to be installed first. Git is an open source decentralized version control system designed to handle every small or large operation with high speed and efficiency—. To install git on your computer, visit the official git website at: consult http://gitscm.com, download, and install it.

Once installed, you can now proceed to install Pyethereum and Serpent. I assume that you know how to use basic command lines. First, type the following command in the command prompt and press the enter key:

```
git clone
https://github.com/ethereum/pythereumbra
nch
```

```
git clone https://github.com/ethereum/pyethereum
```

The above command clones the code that is currently in the ethereum repository and copies it to the local computer. To install Pyethereum, download it from the official website and proceed to the directory in which it has been saved. If you are using Linux, ensure you have launched the Terminal and then navigate to Pyethereum's directory.

Next, execute the following command at the command prompt to install Pyethereum:

```
git branch develop
```

This changes the code to the branch which is more stable and has better compatibility with modern versions of Serpent.

Finally, execute the following command to install Pyethereum:

```
python setup.py install -user
```

Note that the commands may differ depending on the version of the operating system. However, the above commands will perfectly install Pyethereum on your computer if you are using Unix-like operating systems such as Linux and Mac OS.

Next, install Serpent. To install Serpent type the following commands at the command prompt one at a time and Serpent will be installed on your computer:

```
$ git clone https://github.com/ethereum/serpent.git
$ cd serpent
$ git checkout develop
```

SMART CONTRACTS

```
$ make && sudo make install

$ python setup.py install
```

Now that Pyethereum and the Serpent programming language have been installed, you should confirm that they are working correctly. To test your Pyethereum and Serpent, simply navigate to "Pyethereum/tests" directory, type the following command and press the enter key:

```
python pytest -m test_contracts.py
```

Now you are on a good path to become a smart contract developer!

As mentioned earlier, Pyethereum is not the only development framework used for creating smart contracts on Ethereum. You can also use Dapps. However, compared to Dapps, Pyethereum offers more benefits, which is the reason why this book recommends Pyethereum. Below you can find some advantages of Pyethereum when compared to Dapps:

- Pyethereum is simple to learn and use. If you have ever programmed in Python, then you should have no problem with Serpent programming because the Serpent's syntax is similar to Python.
- Pyethereum codes are lightweight and they do not consume a lot of computing power. Serpent compiler was meant to be optimally clean and simple since it combines low-level features and ease-of-use.
- You do not have to install so many frameworks on your computer to begin coding Pyethereum applications. The Dapps set-up environment requires familiarity with all aspects of HTML/JavaScript frameworks such as Web3, JavaScript API, JSON RPC API, and Solidity.

SMART CONTRACTS

Setting up Dapp

We will use the Mix IDE to help you set up Dapp and start writing your smart contracts. Once you finish reading this section, you should be in a position to create your own Dapps in the IDE. The app is available for all OS platforms, Windows, Linux, and Mac OS.

It is important to note that the IDE is in still in the proof-of-concept state. Technology is rapidly changing and, therefore, you should always look for the up-to-date information directly from the official Ethereum website. Before you install the Mix IDE, you should make sure you have installed Turbo Ethereum—C++ Ethereum.

The process of installing TurboEthereum depends on the platform. Currently, TurboEthereum supports three platforms: Windows, Ubuntu and Mac OS X. Let's explore how you can install TurboEthereum on these platforms.

Installing TurboEthereum on Windows OS

Below are the steps you should follow in order to install TurboEthereum on your computer:

- Download the latest version of TurboEthereum from its official website: https://github.com/ethereum/webthree-umbrella/releases.
- Open the directory where the downloaded file has been saved and double-click on it.
- Follow the onscreen instructions to install TurboEthereum on your computer.

Next, install the Mix IDE.

- Download the latest release of Mix IDE from its official website: https://github.com/ethereum/mix/releases.
- Open the directory where the downloaded file has been saved and double-click on it.
- Follow the onscreen instructions to install TurboEthereum on your computer.

SMART CONTRACTS

Installing TurboEthereum on Mac OS X

Below are the steps you should follow in order to install TurboEthereum on your computer:

- Download the latest release of TurboEthereum from its official website: https://github.com/ethereum/webthree-umbrella/releases.
- Open the directory where the downloaded file has been saved and double-click on it.
- Follow the onscreen instructions to install TurboEthereum on your computer.

Next, install the Mix IDE.

- Download the latest release of Mix IDE from its official website: https://github.com/ethereum/mix/releases.
- Open the directory where the downloaded file has been saved and double-click on it.

- Follow the onscreen instructions to install TurboEthereum on your computer.

Installing TurboEthereum on Ubuntu

Below are the steps you should follow in order to install TurboEthereum on your computer:

- Launch the Terminal and type the following commands, one line at a time.
    - sudo add-apt-repository ppa:ethereum/ethereum-qt (When prompted for a password, type your root password and press the enter key)
    - sudo add-apt-repository ppa:ethereum/ethereum
    - sudo apt-get update (this updates your system)
    - sudo apt-get install cpp-ethereum (this installs the TurboEthereum)

Next, install the Mix IDE.

SMART CONTRACTS

Open the Terminal and type the following commands one line at a time.

- sudo add-apt-repository ppa:ethereum/ethereum-qt (When prompted for a password, type your root password and press the enter key).
- sudo add-apt-repository ppa:ethereum/ethereum
- sudo add-apt-repository ppa:ethereum/ethereum-dev
- sudo apt-get update (this updates Ubuntu)
- sudo apt-get install mix (this installs the Mix IDE)
- mix (this command launches the Mix IDE)

Pyethereum smart contract programming assumptions

After installing Pyethrum and Serpent, you should now begin to figure out how you will proceed to the development of smart contracts. However, before you start creating smart contracts, you should first understand the smart contract programming model in Pyethereum. Of course, we have to start with several assumptions, such as the underlying cryptocurrency used.

In this case, we are dealing with Ethereum, which is secure and has a compatible consensus algorithm. It also has monetary value and users gain incentives for using it in smart contracts. The other assumption that we are dealing with is the Blockchain technology that allows nodes in the network to post transactions and other units of the inbuilt cryptocurrency.

The data stored and represented on the Blockchain is guaranteed to be valid according to cryptographic algorithms. The other supposition is that the Blockchain is public. Every node can access a copy of data stored on the block. No node can be prevented from submitting transactions and getting them appended to the

SMART CONTRACTS

Blockchain. There is global agreement about the contents of data stored in the Blockchain history.

Having said that, let's examine other critical assumptions that are necessary for the development of smart contracts.

#1: Contracts and Addresses

The Pyethereum system keeps track of Ethereum currency ownership by linking each unit of Ether with an address. There are two main types of addresses. One is for users—nodes participating in the Blockchain network—and the other for smart contracts. The user address is simply a hash value of the public key, which is a complex mathematical algorithm that produces a fixed value.

Any user who has the public key and the corresponding private key pair can spend the Ether money linked to that address. Users can also create several accounts, as they might want to keep their privacy and prevent accounts to be associated with their real identities.

On the other hand, the contract is any instance of a computer code that can run on the Ethereum Blockchain. All contracts have a program code, storage file, and account balance. Any node in the ecosystem can create a contract by dispatching a transaction to the Ethereum Blockchain. The program code of the smart contract is permanent once it has been developed. It cannot be altered.

The smart contract's code is executed in instances when it receives a message, which can come from a user or from another contract. When executing its code, the contract can also read from or write to any of its storage location. The smart contract can also accept the Ether money into its account and send it from its account to other contracts and users.

Ideally, the smart contract code determines how it behaves when it accepts transaction messages and decides to whom to send money using only contract addresses.

#2: Transactions, Messages, and Gas

A transaction always starts with a message from a node to a recipient address, which can be either another node or a contract. The message must be signed by the user. It can contain data, the ether money or both. Now, if the recipient is a smart contract, then the smart contact code is executed.

On the other hand, if a smart contract code contains an instruction to send a message to other smart contracts, then the smart contract code is executed next. This means that every transaction must always contain at least one message. However, a transaction can trigger multiple messages before it ends.

In this regard, messages act as function calls in any ordinary programming language. After the smart contract has completed processing the message, it can pass the return value back to the sending node. However, in some instances, the smart contract may encounter an exception such as an invalid instruction.

In case of an exception, smart contract control will also be returned to the sending node together with a special return code. In that case, the entire smart contract that includes the account balance and storage location will be reverted to its previous state.

The EVM uses the concept of gas to minimize overconsumption of computing resources. Remember, EVM is handling multiple users whom may be executing several smart contracts. A mechanism must be put in place to minimize the overconsumption of computing resources on the EVM.

Any user who develops a transaction must spend some of the ether money from that account to purchase the gas. During execution of the transaction, every smart contract code will

SMART CONTRACTS

consume some amount of gas. If the gas runs out before the transaction completes, it reverts to its previous state.

Simulating contracts with Pyethereum tester

To test your smart contacts, you have to use the Pyethereum Tester. A Pyethereum Tester is a tool that allows users to test their smart contracts without interacting with the Ethereum Blockchain itself. Testing contracts on a real Blockchain takes a lot of time due to mining challenges when you have to extract enough blocks for your data to be published to the Blockchain and run commands on it.

Therefore, the Pyethereum Tester provides a perfect environment for testing Ethereum smart contracts. To test your smart contracts using the Pyethereum Tester, you have to import it in your code using the syntax below:

```
import serpent
```

```
from    Pyethereum    import    tester,    abi,
utils
```

The above code imports all the assets that are required to run the Tester. Serpent is required to compile the smart contract. From the Pyethereum, you'll need the tester to run all the tests, and the abi to encode and decode the transactions that are appended to the Blockchain. The utilities are necessary for other operations such as generating public addresses.

# Chapter 5

Future of Smart Contracts

Smart contracts are still at their infancy stage and they are still evolving. Even though some applications cannot be legally enforced using smart contracts, they can support contractual agreements and enforce them to some extent.

The mere fact that this revolutionary technology can enforce functional implementations of traditional contracts is proof that these systems will have far-reaching impacts in the future. In fact, gazing into the future of smart contracts helps you take one step closer into science fiction!

Drivers for increased use of smart contracts

Smart contracts with their embedded algorithms not only reduce transaction costs but also create more agile value chains that allow closer cooperation in supply chain management, auto insurance, banking, financial and healthcare industries. Below are the main drivers for increased use of smart contracts in the future:

- ***Minimized risks.*** The distributed process of running transactions eliminates the risk of manipulation since every execution is managed automatically by the whole

Blockchain network, rather than an individual node.

- ***Real-time and accurate record of transactions.*** Smart contracts use algorithms that automate tasks, which otherwise would be performed by manual means. Thus, they increase the speed of business operations and are less susceptible to manual errors.
- ***Elimination of intermediaries.*** Smart contracts reduce intermediaries. In some instances, they can eliminate reliance on third-party companies that provide 'trust' services such as the escrow between trading parties.
- ***They have lower transaction costs.*** Because there is no human intervention, smart contracts have reduced costs.
- ***Generation of new business models.*** Smart contracts facilitate new kinds of business models such as automated access to vehicles and storage units.

Let's explore how smart contracts will affect the following areas:

- Secured Smart Contracts Frameworks
- Data Analytics
- Future law

#1: Secured smart contract frameworks

Amidst new apprehensions about the viability of Blockchain smart contracts, one company has released a system that promotes the security of smart contracts. The Zeppelin project is an open source project developed by Smart Contract Solutions to enhance the security of smart contract applications. The project has an objective to offer community-driven frameworks that enhance secure and audited smart contracts code.

In particular, the authors of the project paid attention to the ecosystem that can be exploited for fraudulent activities. Therefore, the project has the goal to eliminate unintentional loss of funds—

demonstrated by the collapse of Ethereum's largest smart contract (the DAO).

In its development, two sets of tools have been used: Solidity programming language for the creation of smart contract platforms and the Rootstock for future implementations in Bitcoin system. Ultimately, the team envisions creating an autonomous body that automatically rewards smart contract users based on the number of contributions they make to the open-source project.

#2: Data analytics

The potential to link smart contracts to data science is perhaps one of the first steps towards creating a new world of opportunities. Now, with advances in IoT that connects to cloud computing, wireless sensors and physical objectives that include small computer chips, smart contracts can provide that these inanimate objects achieve a certain level of artificial intelligence to work in the 21st century.

The inclusion of data science capabilities to smart contracts may promote self-enforcing financial contracts that execute without a third party. For instance, a farmer can hedge his/her farm produce by using smart contracts which are dependent on various future prices that are computed based on prevailing data analytics.

If the conditions for the smart contracts are met, the system can automatically send payments to the farmer..

However, smart contracts, which enforce data science, may immediately find their potential in digital transfer of goods and services where payment and transfer of payments id is automatic. At the scale that is dependent on the type of contractual agreement, such automation processes may save billions of dollars and improve the efficiency of operations.

However, the use of smart contracts in these areas is yet to be seen. The enforcement of smart contracts and the prevailing laws and regulations in practice still represent a major challenge that has to be resolved in order to achieve the true potentials of smart contracts in data science.

#3: Future law

It is a fact that smart contracts will disrupt several industries when adopted. Smart Contracts, the Dapps, and DAOs are the new buzzwords that disrupt conventional businesses and create a new world order. Smart contracts algorithms and protocols have enacted the "constitution"—which is the underlying cryptographic laws that govern the future world economy. These rules will also change the way people interact with each other in future—through the consensus mechanisms that are used to enforce transactions.

If these smart contract protocols define the constitutional foundations of future civilizations, will they become the lawyers of tomorrow? Basically, these technologies have created "money without the need of banks", "organization without managers" and even "governments without politicians." While all this sounds impossible, it is already here and it is happening right in front of us!

So, if by any miracle you happen to come back to the world in 2100, you will see a different kind of world. You will probably find a world that has "digital lawyers", 'digital judges" and "digital constitutions"!

Chapter 6

Legal Perspectives of Smart Contracts

There is no doubt that smart contracts and the underlying Blockchain technology have been fast-paced, complex and creative. The promise of Blockchain technology is now being recognized by the majority of central banks, financial firms, and governments.

It is expected that this technology will extend far beyond the world of finance and cryptocurrency. The real new revolution has already started with practical implementations in supply chain management, IoT, banking, e-commerce and insurance companies. Nevertheless, not only these industries are revolutionized but law is also being transformed.

The only problem is, as with all disruptive transformations, when technology is fast-paced, complex and ever evolving, the process of separating innovation from irritation becomes intricate and challenging. As more technology is created around smart contracts and Blockchain, we have to rely on our "sixth sense" that will help us separate what is and what is not relevant.

Smart contracts in financial institutions will serve as an example. Commercial litigation organizations are interacting with each other more and more in this area. It is a fact that we are in the midst of a digital revolution, powered by fast-paced, complex and ever-changing internet and Blockchain, which are developing at a scale never witnessed before. I believe that smart contracts and Blockchain technology represent an inevitable progress in the right direction.

What happens to new ideas and legal issues that may crop up in the use of these systems?

New ideas that include legal challenges in accounting and finance will always arise in the use of these systems. For instance, we have already seen some developments in Bitcoins and Ethereum with regard to regulation. While smart contracts are revolutionary, enforcing these in a court of law remains an issue.

The philosophies behind the smart contracts and Blockchain are theoretical. With fewer inputs from the parties that are engaged in contracting, the system is fast and efficient. On this basis, smart contracts can eliminate the transaction costs and ensure efficient operations in the FinTech industry.

However, the only potential challenge is that once you get past the theory and examine the practicability of smart contracts with a "legal mind" you will begin to notice it is difficult to consider them as "smart contracts" or "automated computer codes."

The main objective of establishing contractual terms is to protect personal and commercial interests of the transacting parties. This means a contract is a contingent with two key sources, the prior contractual agreement of the parties and the legal experience, which has an objective to enforce a viable legal contract document.

Now, once that contract has been established, coding may provide continued support for it. The code can even allow minor adjustments, as long as the adjustments are not foreseeable and they are logical. This does not apply to smart contracts.

SMART CONTRACTS

Once the smart contract code has been appended to the Blockchain, it becomes immutable. No alternations can be made to that code, which makes smart contracts one of the most illogical and rigid contractual systems. As a result, smart contracts cannot be relied upon in making complex, binding and sustainable legal decisions that underpin robust commercial contractual agreements.

In addition, the smart contract code works in linear fashion. Therefore, finding the right answer that can settle a particular contractual technicality is more difficult and requires a lot of creativity and flexibility which can only happen in real-life experience.

NOTES

Below is a list of useful smart contracts related resources:

- CoinDesk explores all the things you need to know about Ethereum.
- CIO Articles contain everything you need to know about the Blockchain technology.
- Wall Street Journal delivers everything you need to know about the Blockchain technology.
- Investopedia provides all the details about Blockchain definition.
- Decentralized Autonomous Organizations (DAOs) has all the information about Ethereum.
- Ethereum Blog has all the information about Ethereum.
- Ethereum website has all the information about Ethereum.
- www.law.ox.ac.uk delivers information about legal perspectives of smart contracts.
- Bitcoin Magazine brings about all the information about smart contracts and legal challenges.

SMART CONTRACTS

- Chamber of Digital Commerce provides all the information about smart contract use cases.
- http://ethdocs.org contains all the information about Ethereum smart contracts.
- http://vanderwijk.info/blog has all the information about Pyethereum and Serpent programming.

CONCLUSION

If the internet that we use today is the "internet of information", smart contracts and the underlying technology, the Blockchain, is the "internet of value." Technology enthusiasts have long held the argument that smart contracts hold the promise of curing problems associated with financial contracts, banking transactions, logistics, e-commerce, supply chain management and legal contracts.

Smart contracts and the Blockchain technology have completely disrupted and revolutionized businesses, the world economy, and the society, as we have known. Besides, smart contracts—have created the "decentralized web" and allowed firms to decentralize trust, which is achieved through peer-to-peer network cryptocurrency system.

Before you start to develop the next killer application on the Blockchain, you should understand the concepts behind the smart contracts. That is why understanding the disruptive and revolutionary impacts of smart contracts represent the first step to the survival of your firm in the 21st century.

The main objective of this book has been to explore all aspects of smart contracts that are necessary to learn in order to understand and realize the true potentials of smart contracts.

ABOUT THE AUTHOR

Victor Finch is a zealous enthusiast for the latest technology, innovative gadgets and financial subjects ranging from Fintech to stock trading. These interests strike a deep resonating chord in his passions. He is an entrepreneur, an IT consultant, and a part-time author.

Victor as a child was always fascinated with how things worked; breaking apart his childhood toys is a common sight. Victor always has some innovative workarounds or solutions for his friends or family's problems such as a stubborn laptop that just like to "sleep" and how to improve the quality of life for his family.

If you spot someone, penning down his thoughts while walking down the streets of New York. That could be our dear Victor. He is always intrigued by the latest creativities around and just wants to tinkle with them when he has some me time.

In his spare time, Victor likes to explore the world, read his favorite books, open his little notes and write his next best seller book.

Did you like this book?

If you would like to read more great books like this one, why not subscribe to our website and receive LIFETIME Updates on all our latest promotions, upcoming books and new book releases, and free books or gifts that we occasionally pamper our loyal members.

https://goo.gl/O72cEy

Check out Victor's other proud works below if you didn't get

a chance or follow Victor at

https://goo.gl/y0TVE3

Thanks for reading! Please add a short review on Amazon

and let me know what your thoughts! - Victor

Recommended Read by Victor Finch

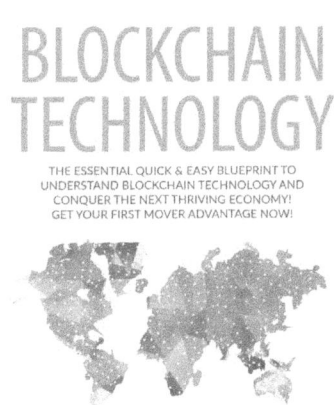

Here are Other Books that You May be Interested In

Discover more books at

https://www.auvapress.com/books

AUVA PRESS

We would like to thank you again for reading this book. Lots of effort, planning and time were committed to ensure that you are receiving the best possible information with as much value as possible. We hope you have unlocked the values from this book.

If you've feel that you have benefited and find that this book is helpful, we would like to ask for a small favor.

Please kindly leave a positive review on Amazon or your favorite social media.

Your review is appreciated and will go a long way to motivate us in producing more quality books for your reading pleasure and needs.

- END -

www.ingramcontent.com/pod-product-compliance
Lightning Source LLC
Chambersburg PA
CBHW061147180526
45170CB00002B/653